THE HISTORY OF THE
COLORADO
ROCKIES

WAYNE STEWART

CREATIVE EDUCATION

Published by Creative Education, 123 South Broad Street, Mankato, MN 56001

Creative Education is an imprint of The Creative Company.

Designed by Rita Marshall.

Photographs by AllSport (Brian Bahr, Stephen Dunn, Otto Gruele, Tom Hauck),

Icon Sports Media (David Seelig), SportsChrome (Jonathan Kirn, Rob Tringali Jr., Michael Zito)

Library of Congress Cataloging-in-Publication Data

Stewart, Wayne, 1951- The history of the Colorado Rockies / by Wayne Stewart.

p. cm. — (Baseball)   ISBN 978-1-58341-207-7

Summary: Highlights the key players and important moments in the history of the

team that brought major league baseball to Denver in 1993.

1. Colorado Rockies (Baseball team)—History—

Juvenile literature. [1. Colorado Rockies (Baseball team)—History.

2. Baseball—History.] I. Title. II. Baseball (Mankato, Minn.).

GV875.C78 S84 2002   796.357′64′0978883—dc21   2001047861

9 8 7 6 5 4 3 2

DENVER,

COLORADO, IS A CITY WITH A RICH HISTORY DATING

back to the early days of the American West. Known as the "Mile High City," Denver sits in the foothills of the Rocky Mountains, giving residents easy access to such outdoor activities as skiing and hiking. Those scenic mountains also provided a name for the professional baseball team that settled in Denver in the early 1990s: the Colorado Rockies.

In baseball terms, the Colorado team is still a baby. In 1985, major league baseball decided to expand, adding two teams to its existing 26 clubs. Six years later, it was announced that the new National League (NL) teams would be established in Miami and Denver. In 1993, after much planning and building, the Colorado

DON BAYLOR

Rockies kicked off their first season.

{THE BIRTH OF A TEAM} Once Denver got the go-ahead to organize its team, the franchise's first step was to find a place to play. Ground-breaking for a new stadium took place in 1992, but that facility, Coors Field, would not be ready until 1995. Therefore, it was decided that the Rockies would play their first two

In **1992**, the Rockies' ownership team paid $95 million to add their new franchise to the NL.

6 seasons as tenants in the Denver Broncos' football arena, Mile High Stadium.

The Rockies' second step was to find a manager. The team's general manager, Bob Gebhard, brought in former big-league out-fielder and designated hitter Don Baylor for the job. It was a risky decision since Baylor had never managed a professional team at any level, but the decision would prove to be a good one. "I didn't know if he could manage," said Gebhard, "but I thought if there ever was

JUAN URIBE

Infielder Eric Young added speed to the **1993** Rockies line-up, stealing 42 bases.

ERIC YOUNG

an opportunity for someone to step into a manager's role and

learn, it would be with an expansion ballclub. So I took a chance

with Don. . . ."

Gebhard then pulled the first Rockies roster

together through various means. First, Colorado

selected a handful of players from other major-league

teams in an expansion draft in 1992. Most of the

players available weren't exactly stars, but it was a start. Three of   **9**

the team's picks, all infielders, would play big roles for the Rockies:

Eric Young, Charlie Hayes, and Vinny Castilla. Then, Colorado took

part for the first time in the annual June amateur draft. In that

draft, the team began building its pitching staff by selecting college

hurlers John Burke and Armando Reynoso.

{THE ROCKIES ROLL} The drafts were just the start of

Colorado's building process, however. At Denver's high elevation,

CHARLIE HAYES

Utility man Terry Shumpert was part of a tough Rockies infield in the late **1990s**.

TERRY SHUMPERT

the air is thinner, which means that baseballs travel almost

10 percent further than they do at sea level. With that in mind,

Gebhard and Baylor looked to add some power hitters to knock the ball around.

Early in 1993, the Rockies signed one such slugger: first baseman Andres Galarraga. Galarraga was certainly powerful, but the "Big Cat" actually earned his nickname with his cat-like agility on defense. The big first baseman told reporters that he signed with the team in part for a chance to play under Baylor. "He was a friend I could talk to," Galarraga said of the manager. "When he brought me here and told me I was his first baseman, I told myself I couldn't let him down."

Galarraga didn't disappoint. In Colorado's first season, he smacked 28 home runs and won the NL batting crown with a .370 average. He would also lead the NL in RBI in 1996 and 1997, with

ANDRES GALARRAGA

his 150 RBI during the 1996 season setting a Rockies record. "He's

a great player, both defensively and offensively," said Vinny Castilla.

"He gives a lot to a ballclub. He's a big presence in the clubhouse

and keeps everybody loose."

Another standout during the Rockies' inaugural season was

hard-hitting outfielder Dante Bichette. Bichette, who was acquired via Colorado's first major trade, would roam the Rockies' outfield for seven seasons. Over the course of his Colorado career, the 6-foot-3 and 225-pound Bichette would collect 1,278 total hits, including a team-record 219 in 1998.

Other players also put forth impressive performances during the Rockies' first season. Pitcher Darren Holmes notched 25 saves, second baseman Eric Young blazed around the base paths with 42 steals, and third baseman Charlie Hayes blasted 25 home runs and collected 98 RBI. The Rockies went 67–95 that season, a respectable showing for an expansion club. Their victory total was actually better than three other NL teams that year.

{WILD ABOUT THE ROCKIES} Other players stepped forward to play major roles in Colorado's second season. These included slick-fielding shortstop Walt Weiss, catcher Joe Girardi,

Starting pitcher Marvin Freeman posted an NL-best 2.80 ERA in the Rockies' second season.

14

DANTE BICHETTE

and pitcher Marvin Freeman. With their contributions, the Rockies

jumped to a respectable 53–64 record during the strike-shortened

season, finishing just six and a half games out of first place in the

NL Western Division.

Hoping to continue their climb up the standings, the Rockies

added right fielder Larry Walker in 1995. The move turned out to be a brilliant one, as Walker drilled 36 home runs and drove in

101 runs in his first season with Colorado. Over the course of

his first six seasons with the Rockies, he would hit

an amazing .339 with a high of .379 in 1999—an

average that stands as an all-time team high and

earned him his second straight NL batting crown.

"He's better than one of the best," Atlanta Braves

manager Bobby Cox said of Walker, who also boasted one of the

strongest throwing arms in the league. "He *is* the best."

In **1995**, third
baseman
Vinny Castilla
became
the third
Colorado
player named
an All-Star.

Vinny Castilla also enjoyed a breakthrough season in 1995,

adding even more power to the Rockies' vaunted long-ball attack

with 32 home runs. Castilla—who was one of the greatest players in

baseball history to hail from Mexico—established himself as a true

star in the seasons that followed, hitting 40 or more home runs

every season from 1996 to 1998.

VINNY CASTILLA

Third baseman Jeff Cirillo manned the "hot corner" after Vinny Castilla's departure.

As expected, pitching was Colorado's biggest weakness in the team's first few seasons, as opposing hitters also took advantage of

Reliever Curtis Leskanic spent seven seasons (**1993** to **1999**) in Colorado, playing in 356 games.

the thin air in Coors Field. Still, right-handed hurler Kevin Ritz managed to win 11 games in 1995. Curtis Leskanic also established himself as a quality reliever as Colorado finished with 77 wins, its best victory total yet. The surprising Rockies finished in second

place in their division—just one game behind the Los Angeles Dodgers—and made the postseason as the NL's wild-card team.

In the playoffs, the Rockies squared off against the NL's team of the '90s: the mighty Atlanta Braves. Colorado fought valiantly in the best-of-five showdown, but the Braves were too powerful, winning in four games and eventually winning the World Series. Still, the hard-hitting Rockies made an impressive showing, with three players batting over .400 during the series: Bichette (.588),

CURTIS LESKANIC

Castilla (.467), and Young (.438).

Despite the playoff loss that followed it, the 1995 season was

a huge success for Colorado in a number of ways. It had taken the

Rockies just three seasons to reach the playoffs (no other expansion

team had ever made the postseason before the end of its eighth

season). For his team's amazing run, Don Baylor was named the NL

Manager of the Year. "Atlanta is the better club," Baylor said, "but our guys really played hard. This experience is something we hope to build off of."

{IN THE BIG INNINGS} It took only a few seasons for the Rockies to gain a reputation for scoring big and often, especially in Denver. In 1996, Colorado set a major-league record for runs scored in one stadium by racking up an astounding 658 runs at Coors Field—a number that averaged out to more than eight runs per game. Colorado was still a very young franchise, but it was growing by leaps and bounds.

The Rockies, whose slugging lineup was known as the "Blake Street Bombers" because the team's ballpark was located on Denver's Blake Street, destroyed the ball in 1996. Brawny outfielder Ellis Burks had been added to the lineup, making Colorado's offensive attack more powerful than ever. In his first season with

Left-hander Bruce Ruffin was the Rockies' top closer in the mid-**1990s**, saving 60 total games.

22

BRUCE RUFFIN

One of the "Blake Street Bombers," power hitter Ellis Burks drove in 128 runs in **1996**.

ELLIS BURKS

the team, Burks not only pounded 40 homers but also tore up the

base paths, swiping 32 bases to become a member of baseball's

exclusive "30-30" club (a group of players with 30 or

more home runs and steals in a season).

Steady
catcher Jeff
Reed batted
a solid .286
during his
late-**1990s**
career with
the Rockies.

Although the Rockies missed the playoffs in

1996, the team treated fans to a great all-around

showing. Bichette joined the 30-30 club as well with

31 home runs and 31 stolen bases; Young finished with an NL-best

53 steals; catcher Jeff Reed added yet another reliable bat to the

lineup; and Ritz and Leskanic continued to put in strong efforts

on the mound.

In 1997, it was Walker's turn to shine. The outfielder's statistics

that season were simply awesome, as he hit a blistering .366 with a

franchise-record 49 homers. He reached base in 45 percent of his

at-bats and boasted a slugging percentage of .720—the best ever

JEFF REED

in baseball history by a left-handed hitter. For his amazing season,

Walker was named the NL Most Valuable Player (MVP).

As Walker crushed the ball in 1997, the Rockies' other sluggers

did their best to keep pace. Castilla slammed 40 home runs, and

Burks added 32 as Denver went 77–85. "We were all just trying

to keep up with Larry," said Bichette, who chipped in 26 homers.

"We didn't want him to embarrass us."

{MORE BIG OFFENSE} Colorado continued to score runs in bunches in 1998. The Rockies finished the season in third place, giving them four seasons in a row in which they finished third or higher in the standings. Walker again excelled at the plate, Castilla had a monster season with 46 home runs and 144 RBI, and reliever Jerry Dipoto nailed down 19 saves.

A star in the field and at the plate, Larry Walker won three Gold Glove awards in the '**90s**.

27

Another new hitting star also emerged for Colorado in 1998: first baseman Todd Helton. In just his first big-league season, Helton finished with a .315 batting average, 25 homers, and 97 RBI. The studious infielder kept a log on opposing pitchers to learn their tendencies, and it paid off. "Helton will be one of the best hitters, power and average, before his career is over," predicted Houston Astros star reliever Billy Wagner.

LARRY WALKER

New talent continued to rise in Colorado over the next two years. Reliever Dave Veres piled up 31 saves in 1999, pitcher Pedro

Astacio tied the franchise record for victories in a season with 17 in 1999, and shortstop Neifi Perez snagged a Gold Glove award for his amazing defense in 2000. Of these up-and-coming stars, Rockies fans were perhaps most abuzz about Astacio's heroics.

28

"Pedro has acclimated four pitches in his arsenal to work effectively at altitude," noted one Rockies team official. "And more importantly, he wants to pitch in Denver and at Coors Field."

In 2000, the Rockies went 82–80. Leading the way was Helton, who breezed to the NL batting title and flirted with the magical .400 level for much of the season. Taking the field across the diamond from Helton that year was newly acquired Jeff Cirillo, a strong-armed third baseman who had replaced the departed Castilla.

PEDRO ASTACIO

Cirillo was a key addition, but new manager Buddy Bell—who joined the team in 2000—was even more delighted after the season when the Rockies brought in one of baseball's finest pitchers. That pitcher was lefty Mike Hampton, who had led the NL with 22 wins the year before and been named *The Sporting News* Pitcher of the Year as a player for the New York Mets.

Left fielder Jeffrey Hammonds put together an impressive 18-game hitting streak in **2000**.

Colorado inked Hampton to an eight-year, $121-million contract, the richest deal ever given to a pitcher. In his first season in Denver, Hampton won nine games before the All-Star break and became the first Rockies pitcher to be selected to the NL All-Star team. Although Colorado finished the year a mediocre 73–89, the Rockies faithful hoped that Hampton and such rising stars as young shortstop Juan Uribe would help turn the team back in the right direction.

JEFFREY HAMMONDS

One of baseball's elite hitters, Todd Helton blasted 49 homers with 146 RBI in **2001**.

TODD HELTON

Rockies ace Mike Hampton was known as one of the NL's most aggressive pitchers.

MIKE HAMPTON

When the Rockies played their first game in team history

in 1993 before a record crowd of 80,227 fans, it was clear that

Young out-
fielder Juan
Pierre swiped
46 bases in
2001 and
emerged as a
top-notch
leadoff hitter.

baseball had found a good home in Colorado. Since

that time, fans in the Mile High City have enjoyed

watching the heroics of some of the game's greatest

sluggers. As the team approaches its 10-year

anniversary, hopes in Denver remain as high as ever.

JUAN PIERRE

ANDRES GALARRAGA

DANTE BICHETTE

TODD HELTON

PEDRO ASTACIO

JEFF CIRILLO

ERIC YOUNG

VINNY CASTILLA

CURTIS LESKANIC

LARRY WALKER

MIKE HAMPTON

ELLIS BURKS

ARMANDO REYNOSO